The Sound of It

The Sound of It

Poems by **Tim Nolan**

Many Voices Project

The publication of *The Sound of It* is made possible by the generous support
of the Jerome Foundation and other contributors to New Rivers Press.

For academic permission please contact Frederick T. Courtright at
570-839-7477 or permdude@eclipse.net. For all other permissions, contact
The Copyright Clearance Center at 978-750-8400 or info@copyright.com.

New Rivers Press is a nonprofit literary press associated with
Minnesota State University Moorhead.

Wayne Gudmundson, Director
Alan Davis, Senior Editor
Donna Carlson, Managing Editor
Thom Tammaro, Poetry Editor
Kevin Carollo, MVP Poetry Coordinator
Liz Severn, MVP Fiction Coordinator
        Publishing Intern: Jennifer Bakken
        Honors Apprentice: Amanda Reiser
        The Sound of It Editorial Intern: Ann Rosenquist Fee
        Editorial Interns: Janet Aarness, Ann Rosenquist Fee, Susan
            Flipp, Chris Hingley, Amanda Huggett, Steve Lauder, Brittany
            Mathiason, Kellie Meehlhause, Ellie Musselman, Rachel Roe,
            Kristen Underdahl
        Design Interns: Danielle DeKruif, Alison Eickhoff, Angelina
            Lennington, Kristen Wieser, Stephanie Thomas
        Festival Coordinator: Heather Steinmann
Allen Sheets, Design Manager
Deb Hval, Business Manager

Printed in the United States of America.

New Rivers Press
c/o MSUM
1104 7th Avenue South
Moorhead, MN 56563
www.newriverspress.com

For Kate, Elizabeth, Maeve, and Frank

Contents

III.

IV.

Waiting for the Song

No matter what corner of the world—
we wait for that song at dusk—
the one that will tell us how the sun

goes down—how it eases into the ocean—
or slips behind the mountain—or—
silhouettes the singer on that balcony above—

the one who wails in that strange voice to Allah—
or to our own operatic Yahweh—
or to the Buddha—then the song seems

smooth as those stones that rattle
and tumble underwater—with fluid
clicking—like tapping on the skull—

And what about New Orleans?—where
the song comes with the slow clarinet
of Sidney Bechet—and seems to suggest

the strong possibility of getting lucky later?
This same old song travels the world—
the *Going Down to Dusk* song—carried

by our original vocalists—the birds—they
cannot stop themselves from singing—
every chance—every loss—every dusk.

*"For the beginning is assuredly
the end—since we know nothing, pure
and simple, beyond
our own complexities."*

—William Carlos Williams

Who I'm After

I'm after the Hittites, the Druids, the 1932
Yankees. I'm after Socrates, Ibsen, Shaw
(I was almost alive with Shaw). I'm after

Chekhov, the Poles who charged the German
tanks on horseback. I'm after the Greeks
who waited inside the horse at Troy.

I'm after those who lived through
the Potato Famine. I'm on the branch of the old tree
that survived. I'm after the *stegosaurus*.

I'm before Derek Jeter. I'm after Walt and Emily
and Abe. I'm after Mark Twain. I'm before Shania Twain.
I'm after Jerry Lewis—even if I die tomorrow—and he lives.

But with you—I'm before and after at once—
I can't quite figure this out—it's my breath—breathing—
then—somehow—it ends up belonging to you.

Chekhovian Childhood

My childhood was *Chekhovian* because the adults
all had a funny dignity about them—
but despair was as near as the front door—

or the breath taken in but never released—
and they all had *deep souls* and *plans*
they could not share except in total silence.

Then—we would all pause to wait for that
creak of the front door and what would happen next.
When I saw *Uncle Vanya* as a boy—

I thought—"How does he know all about us?"
As if he had to be there when my Uncle Gene
and my Dad—as adults—tumbled around on

Grandma's lawn—an old fight—who would rake
the leaves?—someone said the word—*paranoid*—
someone felt a long betrayal—

my ancient and gentle Uncle Walter broke them up—
like a sensible peasant—shuffling over from next door.
I knew things could happen like this—and—

if you place the rifle above the mantle—
you can expect it will go off—but—
since this is comedy—the bullet must always go astray.

Irish Ears

In all the old photographs, we have immense ears—
so I understand why the Brahmins thought we were

from some other race—a race of listeners, mimickers,
brooding, drinking, fighting *hearers*...

And in the old photographs, we fold our hands in our laps,
the left hand keeps cover on the right. Shall we smile or not?

I don't quite smile, but my eyes are bright, all of us—
my sister, my brother, Grandpa and me—are bright.

He wears a black suit, wire-rim glasses, silver cuff links.
He is dignified. Somewhat remote. Proud. I'm sure of it.

Kathleen is sweet—biting slightly on her lower lip.
Patrick wraps his arm around my shoulder which makes me

feel somewhat protected. I wear a *lederhosen* jacket
my aunt bought in Austria. Silver buttons. A costume.

My Grandpa has the evening paper in his lap—*The Star.*
His hands hold his hands, gently. They love one another.

I am waiting for what comes next—I am suspicious
or bemused or befuddled or just four years old—all at once.

How my bad haircut touches me now. Nothing has changed.
I am still waiting. Listening. Listening for the music

that passes quickly, skips no generation—ever—
and is heard—*most movingly*—by the evolved family ears.

Birthday

My mother calls this morning to wish me a happy birthday.
What am I going to do to mark the occasion? I don't know.

I tell her it's really her day, isn't it? Mine, through no effort
of mine that I can remember. It belongs to her, I say, to my father

and her together, driving late at night, late November, driving downtown,
before any freeways, only quiet streets, the first night of my pressing

ambition, through streets dusted with snow, snow that does not accumulate,
but swirls and rises in the high beams, snow playing in the light,

graceful, wispy, elfin … lost snow, that takes on my character somehow
as she recalls it for me. Maybe I've adopted its character. She gives me

this *Dusting of Snow* each year as an image to locate myself.
She knows I will appreciate how she paused over thoughts of me

to observe this snow, coming and going away, lifted lightly into the air
and spun in perpetual snowfalls around the car, down the quiet streets.

So I am: *He Who Comes Before Winter.* Or: *Boy of the Snow Ghosts.*
It's good to know your birth image. Otherwise, the world seems

wide and random, with nothing there to seize you. Not even mountains.
I am: *The One Who Whispers Before the Great Snowstorm.*

Or: *He Who Speaks a Language Far Away from Spring.*
With emergency all around, the snow still rises and falls, breaks

into airy webs, smoky synaptic halos, around the old Chevy, around them.
I am: *Heavy Sky/Light Snow.* I know. It's always been this way for me.

What Does It Matter?

It matters not at all. Then again—
it's everything.

It matters not at all because we sense it
everywhere when we are full

of yearning. When that happens—nothing
is beside the point—the point being:

sun on the table—motes of dust floating
before us. It matters not at all because

we can always turn toward thought
or memory or the calendar of events.

Then—it's everything again—occupying
the great spaces of whatever landscape.

It matters not at all because—
we are in the ocean of it—

always floating in it—even when
we seem to stand up

to address it directly—
It is shy and bold at once.

It is off in the woods while we
are at home—despairing of its return.

English

I love this knock-about tongue, its
hard consonants and cracks, its
noble vowels, its mothering of empty space.

I love the way that English works
on the seashore among the crabs
and green vowels, the way it bakes bread

with vigor and pounds stones
with venom, its venial and cardinal sins,
its fucking and sucking, its mewling,

all the syllabic sense, its birdwalk
and catwalk and small talk, its feisty
short vowels and long sane vowels,

its mister and mistress. I love speaking
in it and I love lounging in the gutter of it.
The sea of it. The sea of it washing

the edge of the page. Then—the down-to-
nothing of it—the fall-to-love of it—
the silence—then—the sound—

Almost Fifty

These years don't mean as much as we think —
they are merely markers for memories — milestones —

or millstones and the effect of the birthday
is always the same — *here I go* — or — *I must be*

in the deep end of the pool. Now some things slow —
then everything speeds up. I would be

dead if I were this age in Connemarra — 1848 —
or if not dead — ancient and gray, with twelve kids.

I would scrape the dry hillside. Still this is a broad
plain, looking across — there's no one else here —

it makes me understand I could become
strange to myself being both the passenger

and my own luggage on a trip that's been going on
so long I can remember — *again* — just how it turns out.

Cuttings

I used to get such pleasure from cutting
keys at the hardware store—in that

high school job—it was the duplication
of the old worn key on the left—screwed

in its bed—for the new brass blank
on the right—it was the tracing of the ridges

of the old mountain range on a new landscape—
it was—*everything*—the whining machinery—

the flecks of brass—flying and screaming—like
brilliant pollen—it was the final smell of cut metal—

and the buffing of the edges with the wire brush—
so the old door would open—somewhere—

into some return—some dramatic homecoming—
some liaison—it was as if—I was a breeder

of keys—a scientist of the exact copy—historian
of entries—sole deadbolt protector—often—

I would just give the keys away—it was my mission—
that the doors would open—by my—exact magic.

Brussels Sprouts

This is the only way to get the kids
to eat their vegetables—set the oven

at 325°— slice the Brussels sprouts
in half—drizzle them with olive oil—did you

get a baking sheet out?—then sprinkle
sea salt—(it should be French sea salt—

La Baleine—coarse crystals)—then watch
until they brown—at which point—it's almost

as if—*vegetables taste good*—at least
that's what our kids thought once—about

a week ago—which will soon be—*long ago*—
and by that time—their bones will be strong

and broad—when they think of us at all—
they'll think of Brussels sprouts—and how

they tasted—*unusual*—and how surprised they were
to find out—we've gone back—to that green world.

Garlic

Odysseus was saved by yellow garlic—otherwise—
Circe would have turned him into a pig—

the smell of garlic—is the smell—of birth—
is the smell—on my fingers—and its—

medicinal properties—are diuretic—expectorant—
stimulating—stomach and heart—but I think—

it's this long smell of garlic on the fingers—and—
the Greeks—left garlic on a pile of stones—

at the crossroads—for a meal for Hecate—
everyone knows—garlic is powerful—I can

smell it on my fingers days later—*and love*—
what I love—is the way this smell stays—

a long time—the longest smell—and it's not—
perfume—it's real life—and the coming—and the going.

Clean Slate

There's something to be said for bankruptcy—
and confession—the counting down to zero—
the exact Hail Marys—the clean slate.

To rid oneself of all that's gotten in the way—
clearing the brush so the creek can be heard
as a litter of bells in the deep woods.

Just then—the old habits gather around—
smoky and lazy as a pile of cats.
Why change what's so familiar and purring?

A broom supplies its own satisfaction—
whispering across the wide-planked floors.
And the mail anticipates happiness each day—

promising a lower rate—a fresh start—
a pause at a quiet café in Thessolonia.
All the dust to be lost in the soft clapping of erasers.

Then—to arrive at the joy of clear water
in the heavy bucket—the sopping sponge—
this broad stroke of black through all the old words.

One Long Breath

The alert cat waiting to spring.
The birds in the morning trying their voices.
The church bells ringing for the dead.

This *green* in the first weeks of summer.
The girl becoming a woman.
The lonely play of the boy

along the roadside—shooting down the tree.
This breath and this line.
The congressman ready for the camera.

The ancient tree—the last great
elm on the block—coming to life
in an airy moment of wind. The sun

striking through the gloomy day.
The lawnmower. The dusk.
The now of Sunday—this first day.

The airplanes. Now. Now some urgency.
Now some calm. The blue car turning
at the corner. The silverware.

The sinks. A bath at night. And now—
the body and the mind and the spirit.
The heart. And now—the falling off.

The Sound of It

I thought of something today that I thought
would lead me into something—not a poem—
necessarily—but some insight that I could

tell someone else—as in a joke or a quip—
such as the last words of Oscar Wilde—
"Either the wallpaper goes or I go." —something

lasting that might be repeated and would
carry a life of its own and so—carry my life—
as if the words could do that—*the words*—

II.

*"For the fountain of water flows
ever with the water of the spirit,
having the one and only Fish, taken
with the hook of divinity ..."*

    —*Narratio rerum quae in Perside acciderunt*

Beyond the Sign of the Fish

The first wild flowers on Suicide Hill were birdfoot violets.

They blossomed near the rocks and from the rusted ravines.

They pecked through collapsed snow fences and broken sleds.

At the sand works, Mesozoic trucks and steam shovels
    gnawed the earth for sheets of glass.

Looking darkly through: Palestine was a dry place
    where people oiled their feet with myrrh,

and baskets overflowed with scraps of fish and bread crusts.

The river rose at Lilydale, flooding the streets. Water
    seeped into all the basements on the six o'clock news.

There were miraculous clouds, burning bushes, and the Red Sea
    like a wall of Jell-O in the *Children's Illustrated Bible*.

Our priest rode Kramer's donkey on Palm Sunday. Kramer's
    donkey was called *Sam*.

Our priest pretended to be Christ. His bishop pretended
    to be God the Father.

We pretended to be children on the road to Jerusalem, waving
    dry Lebanese palms that came in cardboard boxes.

Sacrilege was the brother of *Incense*. *Delusions* were
    bodily sores. *Grandeur* was a French candy wrapped
    in gold foil.

The sun turned with pensioned calm toward green. Poplars
    cast bright shadows on the red Quonset huts.

Where I ran and ran from the boy with the plastic arm.
    He snapped his silver hook, flexing a cord in his shirt.

He pretended to be a pirate. I pretended to be afraid.
Our priest was sent to Iowa where priests were sent
    to dry out.

My sister braided her palm branch in a circle
    and pinned it to her bulletin board.

The sun is turning. Broken in the maple boughs were those
   rustling kites named "Dive Bomber" and "Clipper Ship."

The waters closed in over me, the deep was round about me.

Thunder in the morning. Thunder in the afternoon. The sky was green.

Mr. Bleedhorn called a fire drill and lifted
   his sharkskin jacket off the hook.

Confusion in the cloakroom. Buckles on the boots. Buckles
   on the yellow slickers.

Down the temporary wooden stairs, in the temporary suburb,
   with temporary dread.

Elm branches floated in the baseball hollow. Our voices
   echoed under yellow rain hoods.

*Weeds were wrapped about my head at the roots of
   the mountains.*

We waited in line hoping the Quonset huts
   would burst into flames.

We waited … hoping God the Father would tip a great
   galvanized pail, a pail with red billboard letters
   spelling FIRE.

All thy waves and thy billows passed over me.

Mallards flew across the lining of my slicker.

Hunters drew their beads but never fired.

We waited for a sign as we stood in our Boys' lines
   and our Girls' lines.

Then, they called us back to the warm lights, the white
   paste and a kind of sleep in the afternoon.

At home, I put my ear to the linoleum and heard
   the workings of the house.

My sister said it was Satan. I heard the mechanics of Satan
   cranking the metal pipes with their tails.

An angel from Ewald Brothers' Golden Guernsey woke me.
 Bottles clicked in the wire rack as he snapped
 his metal route book shut.

Our priest wore a linen vestment with an orange sun
 flaming across his chest.

He rode Kramer's donkey sidesaddle and lumbered
 up the aisle like a god.

When he opened his arms to form the cross, this seemed
 a sign or a declaration in some ancient tongue:

"I am, I am, I am that I am," out of the belly of Sheol.

And the Lord spoke to the fish. That was Jonah's sign.

Bridge

Downstairs they are playing *Bridge*. For this game they need card tables, although he can't understand why. He imagines the men on one side of the room and the women on the other side. The women have kicked off their shoes and wade in the wool carpet like little girls. The men take the game seriously and keep their shoes on. Now they face each other, husbands and wives, and they all seem to swallow the silence that floats above the room.

When his family drove in the country and came upon those metal suspension bridges that looked like Jungle Gyms, he always thought the car would go up and over the silver hump. Bridges and roller coasters vaguely resembled one another, in the way Bob Hope vaguely resembled Hubert Humphrey. And so their functions must be nearly the same. Because he closed his eyes and held his breath when they approached one of those bridges, he always figured the car had been safely delivered, up and over the bridge. Across the Rum River or the Red River or the St. Croix.

And so the game of *Bridge* downstairs. The men and women raise their arms above their heads and lean toward one another until their hands touch. Then one of the smaller women walks slowly up the back of one of the husbands. Up and over and slowly down the back of one of the wives. Then they change partners, to see if they are married to the right person, the person who will be able to support them over the swirling wool carpet. This is *Bridge*, and it goes on all night, punctuated by good-hearted laughter. Up and over. Or falling. Sometimes falling into the water like two fish.

Bullhead

We used to throw them back,
disgusted with their prominent
white skulls, bulging eyes,
black shoestring whiskers.
They deeply offended our sense
of what a fish should be. Dirty
scavengers, eating everything
off the sludge bed. They seldom
played on the line, but took bait
with a heavy, impolite thump,
their white bellies rolling
toward the boat. They slid out
of water like drenched birds
snarled in seaweed, their mouths
bleeding from the hooks. Always
we threw them back, down to Hell
where they would think to rise again.

Spearfish

Carl Dobkins' only hit, "Look, Look, My Heart Is an Open Book," piped through the chrome grill of the car radio. They were driving into Spearfish, South Dakota. At Reptile Gardens, his sister had become pale as the man with the microphone taunted the rattlesnake. He kept saying, "Whatza matter … whatza matter?" And his voice seemed to come directly out of his chest, because he hardly moved his lips. His sister went pale because the man frightened her.

In the Chevy, his father smoked Pall Mall cigarettes. His mother was pregnant and wore a striped summer dress that reminded him of that curled Christmas candy that always broke at the bottom of the jar. Carl Dobkins sang, *Look, look, my heart is an open book. I love nobody but you.*

He knew all the words to "Look, Look, My Heart Is an Open Book," because Carl Dobkins was getting a lot of air play. *Some jealous so-and-so wants us to part. That's why he's telling you that I've got a cheatin' heart.* Even when Carl Dobkins stopped singing, the boy kept singing in the back seat of the car as they drove into Spearfish, South Dakota.

He sang "Look, Look, My Heart Is an Open Book" until his brother hit him and told him to shut up. His mother told his brother not to say "Shut up." His brother whispered, "Shut up." He did shut up. But Carl Dobkins kept singing in his mind: *Look, look, my heart is an open book. I love nobody but you.* The singing in his mind went on all afternoon and into the evening. Carl Dobkins sang at the motel, at the diner, and later at the amphitheater where the Black Hills Passion Play was given.

Carl Dobkins sang when Jesus rode into Jerusalem, when Judas tossed the coins across the stage, when Pilate washed his hands. The sky became deep blue. The stage was lit by burning torches, and the Black Hills themselves seemed to gather around the light like slow-breathing animals, reclining on their haunches.

He knew when the camels and the llamas and the elephants trooped out on the stage in an exotic procession, when Christ rolled back the stone and stood in a radiant white robe, that even Christ had to be singing "Look, Look, My Heart Is an Open Book," because the compulsion was that great.

The place was called Spearfish because Christ was speared. And Christ was a fish with a heart that opened like a book.

Holy Thursday

Holy Thursday was the worst about to break — a death that made noise in the attic and kept him from sleeping. This could not last the night.

He wondered which nun dressed the marble family in purple and covered their heads with hoods. Did the same nun do this every year? What were her thoughts?

His mother grew violets under an ultraviolet light on the front porch. When he ran his fingers across the fuzzy leaves, he thought of caterpillars inching their way along the ridge of his arm. He thought of Mrs.Hoffman's moustache and her church — that big building downtown with the black letters three stories tall. SOUL'S HARBOR. He thought of all the souls coming out of their trees, dangling above the sidewalk, dropping to the concrete, and inching their way downtown on thin, transparent lines. The sun never shined at SOUL'S HARBOR. Everyone arrived wet and tired, as if returning from a long and terrible voyage.

He thought of the Shriner's Circus and the funny men who kept coming out of the little car. They couldn't stop themselves. Their honking, persistent arrivals scared him, because he thought — *Enough. There are enough.*

Torn

The curtain of the temple was torn in two. And the ground shook. And a great silence descended like the silence at the center of a storm. We watched the sky through layers of snapshot negatives. Sister Lucia said the sun would burn your eyeballs out and you would be blind for life if you watched the eclipse with the naked eye. The *Naked I* was that figure disrobed on the cross, nailed to wood, looking upward as we were.

The shadow of the moon slowly crossed the prairie and entered the western suburbs. Soon it would be on Lyndale Avenue over Thompson Lumber, over Preferred Risk, over the Mount Olivet Home. Soon it would be over the playground where we stood watching the sky through layers of snapshot negatives.

The moon was eating the sun like an egg snake unhinging its jaw and wrapping its head around the white calcium globe. Sister Lucia said a million moons would fit inside the sun if the sun were a giant fishbowl and the moons were dried peas.

It is finished. The curtain of the temple was torn in two. The moon was a blank disc. Behind it, the corona of the sun pulsated and shot flames. The stone was in place. Sister Lucia said the birds knew to quiet down and wait it out. The wind died in the branches of the poplars. Our voices became muffled and remote as if we each stood at the bottom of our own deep well, as if we each heard the water splashing and the echo of the water. *Pisciculi.* Little Fishes. Swimming beneath the shadow disc of a round, watery surface.

Now on Saturday Within the Tomb

Red wine in a thick-lipped glass that is set beside
    an ashtray that is set beside a book. The book is closed.

This is where you lose the ability to swim in a school.
    You lose the after-dinner talk, the Latin phrase,
    the joke about a nun and a priest.

On the bottom of the glass it says *500* and *Made in France*.
    The glass is beveled with arched faces like bank-teller windows.

The sun is turning. People keep stealing Pathmark shopping
    carts. They leave them forgotten in hedges, in backyards,
    on sidewalks, at stop signs.

You turn the TV off just before they get Caesar at the Senate
    in the City of Rome. He will fall in a bloody heap
    under the statue of Pompey. You don't want to see it again.

The kids upstairs call that squirrel *Rudy* and throw peanuts
    from their bedroom window. Rudy is almost tame
    and lives in the magnolia tree.

Now you lose the desire to be sincere. You lose the parable
    of the mustard seed and the vision of a meadow
    in Harper's Ferry, West Virginia.

You pretend to be tired. You pretend to be distracted.
    You pretend to be a hibernating animal.

But the sun is turning. Last night you dreamed of goldfish
    in a marble pool. You dreamed of a wise man who spoke
    the words, "I am the Door," and wrote those words
    in black Magic Marker on a Styrofoam minnow bucket.

The river rose at Lilydale flooding the pungent root cellars.
    Mason jars floated off the shelves and broke when the water left.
    One week later, everything dried to dust.

Your body holds forty-two quarts of water in a saline
    composition just like the oceans of the Earth. You are
    sixty percent this transparent motion, ebbing and flowing
    through cell walls.

Remember your first homework—*Why We Need Water*—with
  magazine clippings of orange juice, umbrellas, potted
  plants, Charlie the Tuna, a baby in a bathtub, mountain
  lakes, cumulus clouds?

Your conclusion was simple and abstract—a blue pond drawn
  in tilted perspective that was meant to suggest an oasis
  surrounded by white sands. Your conclusion was
  we need water because of thirst.

Thirst being that force that drove you across the lawn,
  around the house to the side yard, where you gulped
  that warm and rubbery water from the green garden hose.

Then you reached a meditative calm. After the black shadows
  passed before your eyes, after you felt the fullness
  of your gut, you saw the landscape clearly—the grass
  and trees, the bright-colored houses, and the sky
  that was tilted like your pond with trees lining its shore.

That was sloshing content. Now the sun is turning above
  the tomb of Saturday. The infant covered in purple
  is ripening in his mother's arms. He is a plum
  about to burst. Out of the water and into the air.

III.

"… but until now I never knew
that fluttering things have so distinct a shade."

— Wallace Stevens

The Breakthrough

After all the days of newspapers—
there were no more days—

with the weather and the news
of Madonna or Patti Page—

there were no more days—
of the president and the congress—

the congress that could accomplish
nothing in the days it had.

There was no more time
for anything that could be planned

for another day—there were no more
days for stacking the newspapers to keep

the time right here beside this time—
which is the only time—*right now.*

There were no more days—no more
papers to count for the days.

That was the time of the flood—
the famine—the genocide—the time

of the endless drought—the insect
invasion—the odd flu that took

everyone in their days—that was
the time of the long war—

the war that went on until it ended—
and then it was gone—and the boys

were never the same again—and
the light was never the same again—

but then—the breakthrough—
which began with a storm in the brain—

a storm that was pressured by all
the days leading up to that day—

which began with a paper and the news—
and that light shining through old glass.

The Lost Work

Last night in a dream—I wrote a Tolstoy epic—set in my time—
all the details—exact—just right. There was an entire chapter

about the dull sound of marbles rolling across the linoleum floor.
Then—the desire for water became a recurring theme, which led

to some confusion about the sex scenes—many of which took place
in frothy hot tubs at a Motel 6 just outside of town. I had to

rewrite—forever—the part where Death showed up at the corner bar—
she finally wore a black satin gown—drank warm tap water from a goblet.

The protagonist's devotion to aspirin did not go unnoticed—that—
along with his compulsion to frequently change the furnace filters.

When the terrorists arrived, they arrived unexpectedly—as expected—
yet—who would think they would wear the various faces of my cousins?

The epilogue ended up being far too long—much longer than the book itself—
which caused me—*to remember*—how much—I wanted to know the end.

The Kids Watching *Citizen Kane*

We told them it was the number one all-time great movie and suggested
they notice the deep focus with Agnes Moorhead in the foreground,

severe and determined, while Charlie plays in the snow out the distant
window, the window that somehow does not seem distant at all since everything

happens all at once here with the inevitable storyline pitching forward and
back at the same time, making the memories within the movie belong to us.

We say keep track of all the ceilings. What other movie has ceilings?
Or cameras in the floor. Her face is hard and his is soft across the widening

breakfast table to indicate the distance that is drawn, we don't say that, exactly,
within the marriage. We don't want to make them film critics, necessarily,

rather help them to appreciate the little things that make watching the mind
a pleasure. Notice how they all talk over one another in herky-jerky dialogue,

just like us, with our odd pace, our odd insights that come at once and must
be quickly said before we forget them or don't notice anymore. Frankie

falls asleep on the couch with the question of whether Charles Foster Kane
gets elected governor, the question dangling there with his sweet breath.

While the girls try to figure out the exact meaning of a *love nest,* the scandal,
whatever, must be someplace for people to sing together to one another

because they're friends, or whatever, with a piano in the corner and heavy drapes.
The girls can't keep their eyes off the screen. They can't turn away from

the art of it and everything that makes the world beautiful and tawdry at once.
The gin and sadness and the blinking neon and the torch-song dead end of it.

Beautiful as long as we can be bright witnesses in our long lives watching
what closely matters, including, but not limited to, the beautiful rosebud

always on the verge of blossom, right next to our heart and the source of our
own voice, might as well be our own soul. In the cold air. Down the white hill.

Frank, Running Around the House

He's in training for some baseball game
a long way from this winter — and who

would want to go outside now anyway? —
when your breath — crystallizes — and drops

to the sidewalk — like a scattered wind chime.
He says — *How many times around the house*

is a mile? — (About sixty times) — and so
he runs sixty times around inside the house —

(smiling at me each time) — like a happy baby —
(Oh — How can we survive this beauty?) —

pushing ahead — with diligence that I
no longer have — (never had) — but once

remembered — (it all comes back again) —
circling around the stove — cutting past

the pantry door — into the curve
of the living room — around the sofa again —

and then — the white refrigerator wall —
with the little pictures and sayings there —

with everything held up by realtor magnets —
the pavement of linoleum — the pounding feet —

this — insistence of the body moving — this
insistence — come from me — turning again.

Elizabeth Playing "Für Elise"

You've gotten past the toodle-
doo business to the deep
and insistent bass, which is

real life and emphatic.
That's what's great about
Beethoven—not that I know—

but it's just that the pounding
storm is never far away
from the lyric melody—

and so—the notes might never
run out. Or else—they might
be smashed on the rocks.

Then—we're back to the toodle-
doo and a pasture
with cows and grass.

The cows are then pounded
against the rocks. The cows
don't even know they've been

killed—as they float above
those bass notes. Exactly
where they want to be.

Memory Too

When you get to be a certain age—anticipation relaxes
and you sense the past as a long-tailed comet and you

(your face like a fat snowball) the flaring trajectory
at the head of it—with deep space out in front of you.

Then—sometimes—pausing over the puzzle—you realize
your mother's maiden name is odd—*Leadon*—weighted down—

yet somehow free—depending on your pronunciation.
And once in awhile—a whole scene comes back—

a quiet room—the afternoon light—then a slow-moving cello
tapping its way on the stairs—taking its long breaths at each landing.

Of course—you always rearrange the sequence of events
to place yourself at the very center, always getting in the last word—

rising from your chair to speak the final paragraphs of *The Great Gatsby*.
Even embarrassment—even despair—take on that nostalgia of the scar—

that accommodation on the surface of the skin. And your body
becomes an easy suit—made of that durable and yet-to-be

discovered fabric that changes color and texture—expands
and recedes—not at your command—but somehow—of your willing.

Diamond Lake Bowling

In the seventh frame projected
on an overhead screen, my father,
Pat N., has a 180 working on a spare.

My mother, Marge N., is just ahead
of Gladys P. and far ahead of Yvonne K.,
who sings in the church choir and doesn't

take this game too seriously. My mother,
Marge N., doesn't take the game
too seriously, but she has a 158

working on a strike, which is fine,
and seems to be enough to beat
Gladys P. and Yvonne K. My mother

wants to beat them by a narrow margin—
enough to win—but not upset their society,
which matters among them most of all.

The men—Bill P., Jack K., and my father,
Pat N., are serious bowlers. They each
release the ball in their own ways,

with controlled madness. Then they wait
for lacquered thunder to come crashing
down like museum skulls. What a mess!

The women approach the line with quick,
tentative steps, as if they were naked,
covering themselves, then letting go.

Yvonne K. sings "Ave Maria" at funerals.
Makes everyone weep. Here, she is
without talent and gets no action

from the pins—which slowly fall
in soft and mid-age stupor.
My heart echoes in a memory cavern

as I gaze at the blue and broad
Hollywood curtain along the sidewall.
My parents turn to me across the way.

Dear lively eyes of them. My first faces.
Always surprised to see me.
How can I explain this sense, become

serious, that we are picking up speed,
rolling in upon ourselves, and falling
alone down this noisy, inevitable lane?

The Museum of Russian Art

I'm not kidding—it's coming to our unlikely neighborhood—
at the corner of 35W and Diamond Lake Road—they are
building—*The Museum of Russian Art*—in the old Mayflower

Church—which later became—*The Enga Funeral Home*—so—
there are spirits enough—imbedded in the plaster—enough
spirits—and voices—to hover around the deep jeweled mystery—

of *The Black Madonna*—or—Christ Pantocrator—with all the gold
surrounding the faces—to focus the devotion of anyone looking—
or—they might have Kandinsky's funny horsemen—stepping up—

that *Blue Mountain*—or why not a Fabergé egg—right here—
in South Minneapolis—opening under our eyes—*unclasped?*
I have this dream—I'm a fidgety old man—wanting to move—

so I walk down Diamond Lake Road—*along the Diamond Path
of the Czars*—to the roaring freeway—and none of the noise will
bother me—it will be just like the locomotive—screeching—

to a stop—*The Astapovo Station*—where the old man had to get off—
now freed of his bed sheets—*now on that final quest*—to get away—
that itching of life—to get away—where?—where faces are lit in gold.

50

Elizabeth's Friends

Came over today—with boots & chains
& green hair—but they are lovely &
sweet—calling me "Mister."

And lately—Elizabeth is blond—her hair
is really as yellow as the Dutch Boy's—
& she's attentive to me in a way

she wasn't a few weeks ago—*I'm not
so old*—she sometimes thinks & so
do I—& this we have in common.

Now they are playing angry songs
on the computer—but their faces are
beautiful—listening—waiting for me to leave.

Grief

When I was alone in that small room
I seemed to bounce off the walls.

The narrow bed was the size of a coffin.
The springs creaked as my dreams turned over.

I would come down to nothing — not
a voice or word — nothing but surface

reaction. I had not yet gathered
my habits. I had no beliefs that held.

We were all inmates there in the TV room
with the World Series blaring. George Brett.

Mike Schmidt. It did not matter whoever won.
I was among sad men who never expected much.

Then — some reassembly or chiropractic
adjustment occurred over time with me.

This yearning to be a mammal would be hard.
Tears and panic. The flight and the descent

from the trees to solid ground would take years.
I saw the clouds coming in over the river.

The moon was contained in an apartment window.
It was enough — one day — I came down to that.

Meteor

Around the fire we sang
Hank Williams' songs
about our cheatin' hearts
and what we got cookin'.

The great river was behind us.
The train to Chicago
split the night with a long
soulful moan. Where

are we going? Just then
in search of the Little Dipper,
it flashed above our heads.

Spiking the atmosphere—
a ball of hot iron—
that sizzled and sparked
as it shot into our realm.

From elsewhere.

We heard it.

We smelled the burning down.
Whatever remained
landed on a pinpoint
in a field
beyond the ridge
knocking
a ladybug
off
a
leaf.

The
rest
of
it
landed
in
us.

Full Stride

I'm watching *Antiques Roadshow* where
they're looking at a clock by Samuel Mulliken

that is worth $75,000—while our oldest daughter
is roaring through "Rhapsody in Blue"

on the out-of-tune piano (the F sharp is dead)—
and now they are looking at a print

of a locomotive (The Taunton Locomotive)
that is worth $3800 (not to me)—and now

I'm thinking I should change the channel—
to see what's happening with the war—but

I already know having just read the newspaper—
and now they're examining a porcelain Rembrandt

knock-off of an incredibly ugly woman—and
they say it's only worth $1500—but the frame

is worth much more—without the ugly woman—and
it's Christmas almost—the tree beside me—

dark and fragrant—not lit yet—for a moment
I'm in the deep forest—piled high with snow—

and now our nephew Matt comes over for dinner—
he's going to Iraq next month—we got him

some wool socks—an Orlon T-shirt—and special
goggles that will protect his eyes from shrapnel—

(I can't believe I've written this)—it seems we should
make something of our weariness—some full

breath and quiet out of all the noise—Matt tries on
the goggles and socks—he looks like a yellow-eyed

alien—dressed up for Christmas—he looks like
his grandpa looked—straight at the camera—in full stride.

Prayer Chain

My mother called to tell me
about an old classmate of mine who

was dying on the parish prayer chain—
or was very sick—or destitute—

or it had not worked out—the marriage—
or the kids were all on drugs—and

all the old mothers were praying intensely
for all the pain of their children

and for life—they were praying for life—
in their quiet rooms—sipping decaf coffee—

I bet they've been praying for me at times—
so I'll find my way—so I won't rob a bank—

I'll take them—the mystical prayers of old mothers—
it matters—all this patient and purposeful love.

Something Jotted Down

At 3:30 a.m.—when it seemed to matter—
then later—it looks like—"Ugh valiter"—

something the cat brought in—the cat—
with his beautiful face—and his—*purr*—

And what about the only joke I can ever
remember?—the one about the guy in the bar

with a chicken on the barstool next to him—
and his wife waiting at home—*I love*

that joke—(it's the only one I can remember)
because it reaches a level of malice that tempers me.

And why not focus on the footnotes
in the book about Lincoln's melancholy?—

How his melancholy was immense—and—
creative in the end—in that it compelled him

to further suffering (and laughter)—which
imagination *(real imagination)*—requires.

So—when I wake up again at 4:30 a.m. (now)—
I'm almost used to—the way—I can always hear

the newspaper hit the front door—the news there
on the front stoop—it has become the same news—

(suicide roadside bombs)—Fallujah—and then
flares of regret go off in my heart—*(my heart)*—

which is usually big—sometimes small—
(too often fretful—you know this also)—it's the way

the cold rushing wind arrives like the world—*turning*—
(as it slows)—(turning again)—as it almost seems to stop.

The Party

That was the party where the guy
fell off the cliff above the river
and nearly broke his neck

Or was it the party when the police
arrived with the mayor—the mayor
yelling at us—on a bullhorn—to clear out

I'm thinking it was the party
where the house burned down
next door—we watched it like fireworks

Then—there was that party when
the two girls were kissing under
the winter coats in the bedroom

One time Chris called Ann a *cunt*—
in the kitchen—then he started
sobbing—even as we took him home

There were always too many of us—
at whatever party—the music shook
the walls—someone passed a joint

I was usually more interested
in the small conversation near
the back door—I always felt too old

to be at that party—it was too
chaotic—especially the New Year's
parties—when no one considered—the future

Totally Random

So at last it's summer and I'm driving
my teenage daughter and her friend to the latest
blockbuster movie at the Mega Star Cinema,

and we're chatting in the car about the last
latest blockbuster movie we each saw in the last
week, and Lizzie says — *It was like a monster movie*

with the weather as the monster, and Lizzie and Mary
now dissect the movie in a way that belongs
to fourteen-year-old girls and is very pleasing

to me because they see below the surface of this
Big Culture, and I'm thinking — *Maybe we are*
raising healthy skeptics, even if they are

goofy and loud and easily amused and shyly
knowing, and now they are observing how
totally random it was in the monster weather movie

when the wolves showed up on the Russian freighter
that had eased down Fifth Avenue, scraped its hull,
and came to rest on the steps of the New York Public Library,

how random that the wolves were so aggressive
when they would probably just cower in the cold
and turn in on themselves, *doggishly,* and could books —

even the Gutenberg Bible — burn at all if it was 170° below,
and random, *totally,* how the girl had to slice open
her leg on the bumper of the taxi cab, just so

the boy could search the Russian freighter
for those Russian medical supplies. I said —
they wanted to work in a love story too,

and the girls both go — But that's so random …
And what about the randomness of divorce
in the movies and everywhere — everyone's

divorced and happily divorced and even *in love still*
but divorced and the ex-husband and ex-wife are both
beautiful and understanding parents with beautiful

and wise children who help them find a way
to themselves, and I'm thinking — these girls here
in the car are so smart and alive that I would walk

from Philadelphia to New York City in my snowshoes
and special Arctic gear to save them, but at the same time
I'm thinking — *how totally random,* being in this car,

rushing down Xerxes Avenue so the kids won't miss
the previews, and random the previews and random
the president and the congress, random the transit of Venus,

completely random — the beginning of this endless summer
of being fourteen years old, and *inevitably random*
watching the boys slouching into the Mega Star Cinema,

their baggy pants and rangy wolf-like prowl, and
random my watching, *random* as in — *a random bystander* —
all of this — makes my promise to return later — seem *full* with intent.

Wealth

Down the block a garage band plays
"Isn't She Lovely" —here's a kind of wealth

even if the song is fractured—and listening
tonight to the sequence of birds—I mean

their *unintended consequences*—is wealth—
and today I followed all the plays—each

count around the baseball diamond—no one
expected their due—the *outs* were *out*

and some of the runners were *safe*—there was
sense in the blue sky—it could all go

beyond nine innings—whatever—I mean
everyone agreed and understood this passing—

this endless passing of time—was a kind of wealth—
and our atmosphere would be enough—the trees

would frame the sky and the sky would be
beyond belief—*so blue*—as in *Mediterranean Blue*—

and Odysseus would come home—as he was
compelled to—sunburned, vagrant—and wealthy.

Greenland

For Jack Mulloy

We didn't know where we were going —
except it would be cold. And not green.

We couldn't tell our wives or kids where we were
until much later. The letters and numbers

on the side of the plane were as tall as a man.
One iceberg looked like a Dairy Queen cone.

We built concrete columns eighty-five feet down.
A generator valve snapped off in my fingers with the cold.

If you walked out fifty yards on the ice —
you might not come back. It was *green*

in *Greenland* only in the short spring and summer —
when icebergs slipped off their shelves and floated away.

One guy from New Jersey looked just like the actor
who was married to the woman who had a man's name.

What was her name? What was his name?
He made movies *with what's his name*. What the hell!

Sometimes — we didn't know where we were going
or where we had been. Except by remembering the babies

and the places they were born — Texas, Mississippi,
Wyoming, North Dakota, Minnesota. Train stations

hectic during the war. Our cars broke down.
New babies with us everywhere. *Bring me a new*

baby now. Along with a bowl of cherries. And a pear.
The babies told us where we were going and where

we had been. In letters and numbers as tall as a man.

The Grass

When I let myself calm down —
I come back to the grass —

that evening after dinner — when I
knew I was myself — for the first time.

I lay in the grass looking up
at that summer sky — that

was a lifetime ago — it was
the only lesson that stuck — the grass

tickled my ears — it held me —
and grew around me — and grew

from me — that's when I learned
to pull the flower from the shoot —

for the grass is a flower — must be
the first flower — and when

I pulled the flower from the shoot —
delicately — I could chew that white meat.

IV.

"The wind is thus a breath of air that,
a breath of air which ...
etc., etc."

— Francis Ponge

The Wind

The wind in the giant cottonwood tree
is the same wind across the broad ocean—

and the same small wind through the low grass—
it is—the same wind that ripples the skin—

or blows through the blond infant's wispy hair—
but back to the cottonwood tree—the wind

is particular to each leaf—devoted—and in
its assembly—the wind is magnificent in the tree—

standing for—everything—in time with—everything—
somehow in time with me—as I watch her play

on an old field of my humiliation—it's a moment—
in this long living—when I am here—and still gone.

The Unified Theory

The physicists sought something I don't understand—
a unified theory—to connect everything—
but I sense the problem is not one of *matter*—

that the unification—if there is such a thing—
comes down to *spirit*—and—*intangibles*—
such as the laughter of my son at my small joke—

or the way the yard is so fresh—and *renewed*—
after the rain stops and the sun comes out—
or the way the smart cat in the window watches me

with *intense indifference*—and the place
of unification—if there is such a place—
is somewhere behind my forehead—in my eyes—

seeing out and sorting out—and while there may be
a vacuum in deep space—there is no vacuum
here—in fact—it is this *abundance* that causes

confusion and leads to the desire for order—
and the theories somehow find their way back
to us—because we are *tuned* to majestic chords.

The Big Curve

I can still do the crossword puzzle—
at least until Wednesday—but
on Thursday—I can't remember a word—

or spell anything—I can still run—
when required—but I place myself
in fewer situations where running

is required—If I skinned my knee now—
the rest of my leg might fall off—
and while I've never broken a bone—

if I did—I might give up the wrist—
or the thumb—I would accommodate
the bum ankle. I forget everything—

all the time—the name of Gary Cooper's
wife (why should I know that anyway?)—
or Hamlet's best friend from college—

or even where Hamlet went to college—
I try to remember the new employee's name—
but it always seems to be Alyssa—or Jessica—

or Kristen—(not Kirstin)—why do I need
to remember this anyway?—It makes me
sad to be failing all these tests—

Then—at once—I remember how the bright snow
billowed up and banked the sidewalk on the way
to school—it was different then—how we walked

everywhere—or ran—and when we rode
in a car—it was still a luxury—it was
a magic carpet—the way the capacious

Chevy floated on a cushion of air—so—
when we came to the big curve in the rocky road—
(her name was *Rocky)*—we would lean into

each other—holding that welted cord tight—
leaning into the big curve—not feeling any
bumps along the way—as if—it would never end.

The Eulogy

He could be funny, but only in small groups
of meek women—which is to say—he was not

very funny. He had beautiful and expressive
hands, which he normally kept in his pockets.

When he was roused to passion, as he seldom was,
it would usually go unnoticed. He did have

strong feelings for animals—his family crest included
the loon—that symbol of fidelity and lonely song.

He was quite a mimic—I personally remember
how he could sound just like Bobby Kennedy—underwater—

if he was drunk enough. I suppose you all remember
his obsession with orchids—it was strange at the end—

his fretting over their blossoming—*when would it happen?*
Then, his disappointment when they would fade and drop.

He was a collector of sales receipts—some of you
may not know this—he would ask you to empty

your pockets to show him where you'd been, what you bought.
At his confirmation on June 4, 1954, he chose a verse

from the Old Testament, *The Book of Haggai*—"He that
earneth wages earneth wages to put in a bag with a hole.

Consider your ways, sayeth the Lord." Let us consider
him...as we head downstairs. There must be other stories.

Once in New York

I spoke to Greta Garbo—I said—
"Good evening"—she said—"Good evening."

I was a young man—she was an old lady—
but she was beautiful in her actions—

rushing across the lobby—she was as fleet
as a doe—turning in the dark forest—

wary of everyone in the woods—but not me—
she was not wary of me—I was harmless—

Then I knew the quick connection to something
rare and passing—the only living example—

Helen—long after the Greek men found their way
home—and tried to remember her voice again.

Elephants at the Airport

Their trainers carry wooden prods
and nudge them down the gangplanks.

Six blind men would say a mountain
chain has arrived at the airport

and it is moving. Hannibal floated
thirty-eight elephants on the Rhône

by building jetties and earth barges.
The Gauls watched from the other side

and rallied resistance to new order
plodding toward them. A few elephants

made it up and over the Alps to Italy
where they'd never been. Baggage carts

resemble centipedes, enlarged and manic.
The crazy planes buzz National Cemetery

and skid the rows of blunt headstones.
Now you will understand those devotees

of Vishnu who threw themselves beneath
the Juggernaut, cracking streets in Puri.

Under this thin tarmac, dead soldiers feel
this weightless pressure, a majestic

slowness of elephants in their suburb,
enough to stop all passing clocks.

At the Choral Concert

The high school kids are so beautiful
in their lavender blouses and crisp white shirts.

They open their mouths to sing with that
far-off stare they had looking out from the crib.

Their voices lift up from the marble bed
of the high altar to the blue endless ceiling

of heaven as depicted in the cloudy dome—
and we—as the parents—crane our necks

to see our children and what is above us—
and ahead of us—until the end when we

are invited up to sing with them—sopranos
and altos—tenors and basses—to sing the great

Hallelujah Chorus—and I'm standing with the other
stunned and gray fathers—holding our sheet music—

searching for our parts—and we realize—
our voices are surprisingly rich—experienced—

For the Lord God omnipotent reigneth—
and how do we all know to come in

at exactly the right moment?—*Forever and ever*—
and how can it not seem that we shall reign

forever and ever—in one voice with our beautiful
children—looking out into all those lights.

Based on a True Story

Once we taped up all the corners
in our little apartment and sprayed
insecticide everywhere—and we thought
we got rid of all the cockroaches—
But how could we think that?—
since cockroaches have been around
for about 250 million years—and
in our little kitchen the little radio
was warm and tuned to WNYC—
and the light glowed and the music
of Mozart made us happy—then we saw
that cockroach riding on the yellow dial
down to where the slow dirge came
from New Orleans—to where Phil
Rizzuto said "Can you believe that?"—
when the first baseman couldn't lay down
the bunt—and we opened the back
of the radio and they swarmed out—
(they had eaten the glue behind the knobs)—
and we screamed—*"Oh My God!"*—
we were so disgusted—with all the life
of it—*the incessant life of it all*—
I don't think we're over it yet.

Signal from the Stands

He's a much better athlete than I ever was—
the way he rises on the balls of his feet

before each pitch—and is ready and focused
to move—and the way when the action

stops—he conserves his strength—doesn't
waste a moment—covering first base

with that mitt the size of Rhode Island—
his slender and perfect legs—the crisp

white pants—the way he crowds the plate
and is not afraid of the big dumb pitcher from Blaine.

Then—when he has the time to wait—
the time in the endless summer to wait—

he might look toward the stands—toward me—
and I give him our own signal—that *thumbs up*—

which he acknowledges— across the years—
just for me—this serious nod—from his blue cap.

La Dolce Vita

For Kate

Marcello is called *Marcello* — in the movie — he can only be *Marcello* —
he acts like a silent-movie star — so you don't need Italian to understand

how tired he has become in his life — racing around Rome in his convertible —
trying to keep track of all the women — with his friend *Paparazzo* — the source name

for all tabloid photographers ever since — then — when his *Papa* — his — *Dad* — visits —
Marcello remembers his past and his *Mama* — and how odd he doesn't know his *Papa* —

but wants to know him — and it's all there in his eyes — those silent-movie eyes —
everything he comes to know — there — in his eyes — and the movie must end at the sea —

at the source — after the silly sixties go-go party — at dawn — when the fishermen drag up
a sea monster in a great net — alive — the monster's eyes are alive — that's what Marcello

finally sees — then he sees the beautiful girl — the angel he met earlier — and both —
the angel — and the monster — they both are watching — *with love* — his sweet life.

Talk

Remember—how our talk would go on
all night—to no conclusion—a perpetual
cul de sac?—Our talk might have been

about how we liked the book but not
the movie—how the new building looked
like a giant grandfather clock—sort of goofy—

And it all mattered so much—in a way
that seems naïve now—if not desperate—
but there was a flow to it all—in fact—

our talk followed the continental patterns
of the smallest rivulet—leading to the broad
river of talk—meeting ourselves at that convergence.

The bottle was done. The match
was struck. And from your serious brow—
I knew—the eternity of talk—how it flares.

For My Country in Its Darkness

But it seems as if there's light—
on the television screen—behind
the e-mails—and from the dashboard—

everything is lit—in full sunlight—
but then there's sudden darkness—as if
someone put drops in your eyes—

and said—"See how everything's so nice"—
Even the rooms for torture are lit
like drugstores—with shelves and shelves

of choices—"We could do this to you—
or that—it depends on what you say"—
And our fear is so well lit—

that it almost seems like no fear—
because the sky is blue—the waves
roll in their regular course—while

the trees grow to the height of the house—
it seems as if there's light—
but nonetheless—we are in darkness—

Sleep

I look forward to it—as a destination—
a kind of *Cozumel*—at the end of my day.

There—the warm water laps in—the sky
is that endless blue—and I think—*This could*

be perfect—as the trees sway—they are
palm trees—I think—but they could be

oak trees in *The Great Woods*—along
the Mississippi River—might as well be—

and the snow falls into the dark
water of the river—and the house is lit—

up on the hill—do you realize how
all these dreams are one dream?—

the walls are mirrors—the faces—
one face—looking this way—

The Dreams of the Old

So they are around our table — my mother,
my father, an uncle—and we begin to talk
about our dreams—with some urgency—
as if our dreams could pinpoint our psychic
dangers—our unrealized goals—our
ordinary fear of death and the future.
My mother talks about her dreams of flying
over the little town where she grew up—
over the old Opera House—down Main Street—
with all the people she knew below her—
then towards the gently flowing river—
that seemed to flow into the sunset—
toward which she soared—she lingered
with us on that image—as if she had said
enough—then—my uncle talked about
his recurring dream—he's going to be
in a play—but no one's bothered
to rehearse the scenes—he's standing
in the wings waiting to go on—he doesn't
know what he will say—all through this
my father is silent—he is closest to death—
we all know this—we forgive him his silence—
his silence—has his presence—as in a dream.

Walking Around

You wanted to talk about the big
things—as in what Jesus meant
when he threw out the moneychangers—

and did he have a sense of humor?—
and didn't he seem peevish when
no one understood *"The Kingdom of God*

Is Within"?—we kept talking and talking—
until we were no longer father and daughter—
we were just two of us—knowing nothing—

together—we walked down Pleasant Avenue—
around to Pillsbury Avenue—then around
again—because walking around like this—

calms the mind—and then your voice
became way too loud for our neighborhood—
as you condemned—*The Right-Wing Wacko*

Nutjobs—and I didn't think to quiet you—
as if you were still a baby—those times
when you screamed in the night—

frightened—of nothing—we kept
walking—as we talked—about the big things—
from our hearts—within the Kingdom.

The Future

Will the house be here at all? —
(It won't)—will the children wonder? —

(Where their house went?)—(their
childhood)—and the chimneys—

(like the old plantation houses)—
will stand—while the wood (within)—

is gone—Could the grass be the same
family of grass—(probably)—as now?

And the soil—(with our bones there)—
will it send up (eucalyptus trees?)—

(as if from some Guatemala of our love)—
while the night sky (in early winter)—

remains exactly—*(as it is)*—lonely
and cold (but definite)—with the clouds

rushing over the face of the moon—
as thought—(this slow thought).

The Last

I was the youngest in my family—
and so I beheld that danger—
of being spoiled—*(I was spoiled)*—

and how that spoiling worked on me—
I could see the bright moon
becoming my own lantern down

the long path of my spoiling—
the rotting character—the bratty
insistence—of me—so even now—

so many years after my spoiling—
I can be fresh—there's the irony
of being spoiled—you can come back

fresh forever—as if the process of spoiling
led to something new again—a wisdom—
(my wisdom)—come long—and easy.

Morning Glories

Morning glories climb up the lamppost—
the downspout—the trellis—*morning
glories* — poised to take over

the house—our dreams—*morning glories*—
climb up our spines—wrap
our bodies—*morning glories*—ecstatic

in August—always on the edge of sleep—
this side of frost—*blue*—
as a steady pilot light—and—white—

at the center—as if at the center
there's a memory of snow and cloud—
and when they close—*that blue*—

becomes a wrinkled purple—a different color
altogether—*preserve of summer*—these *glories*—
they must always *close* in the dark.

Acknowledgments

Grateful acknowledgment is made to the following publications where some of the poems in this volume first appeared:

Gettysburg Review: "Full Stride," "Greenland," and "Something Jotted Down"

Great River Review: "Irish Ears" and "Sleep"

Knockout: "Elizabeth Playing 'Für Elise' "

Legal Studies Forum: "Birthday," "English," "Memory Too," "Signal from the Stands," "The Party," "Totally Random," and "The Unified Theory"

The Nation: "Elephants at the Airport"

Pivot: "Meteor"

Ploughshares: "Beyond the Sign of the Fish," "Bridge," "Bullhead," "Spearfish," "Holy Thursday," "Torn," "Now on Saturday Within the Tomb," and "At the Choral Concert"

Sport Literate: "Diamond Lake Bowling"

Tolstoy Studies Forum: "The Lost Work" and "The Museum of Russian Art"

Water~Stone: "The Dreams of the Old"

The Writer's Almanac: "The Dreams of the Old," "The Lost Work," "Prayer Chain," "Once in New York," and "The Eulogy"

Biography

Tim Nolan was born in Minneapolis in 1954 and graduated from the University of Minnesota in 1978 with a B.A. in English. He and his wife Kate moved to New York City in 1978 where he obtained an M.F.A. degree in writing from Columbia University, worked as an archivist at the Whitney Museum, and read the poetry slush pile for *The Paris Review*. Tim returned to Minnesota in 1985 and received his law degree from William Mitchell College of Law in 1989.

He is an attorney with the McGrann Shea law firm in Minneapolis where he practices in litigation, including real estate, eminent domain, and construction. Tim lives in South Minneapolis with Kate and their three teenagers—Elizabeth, Maeve, and Frank.